STAY AWHILE

LYDIA UNSWORTH

Published in the United Kingdom in 2026
by The Knives Forks And Spoons Press,
51 Pipit Avenue,
Newton-le-Willows,
Merseyside,
WA12 9RG.

ISBN 978-1-916590-17-5

Acknowledgements:

With thanks to the editors of *Anthropocene, Culture Matters, Ludd Gang, Pissoir* and *Salzburg Review*, and the *More Song* and *High Rise* anthologies, where some of these poems first appeared.

This project was supported by an Arts Council DYCP grant. Thanks to Fran Lock and Tom Branfoot for their enthusiasm and edits. Much gratitude goes to Jen Orpin for letting me use her beautiful image 'The Last Landmark' for the cover of this book. And thank you to Alec of Knives Forks and Spoons for publishing my work once again.

Contents

Verweile doch, du bist so schön

– Goethe, *Faust*

Now that you've wasted your life here, in this small corner,
you've destroyed it everywhere in the world

– C. P. Cavafy, 'The City'

When we build again, we must not repeat our old mistakes

– Lynsey Hanley, *Ground Control*

STAY AWHILE

FFS

It's like, *you built this*. You don't just get to say *I quit* and start again like you're 77 and can father a new family without consequence any time you feel up to it. You built this and you leave it behind. The guardians say *no* while you try to cut it out like circles from a tight orange dress. But who listens to a guardian? We've got the loud man here. And he's outwitted us again because in the rules, rules he wrote, it says culture is the hand around the wrist.

Crewe (60p return)

I decided to stop feeling sorry for myself
and bought a bunch of tickets
in the #NorthernRailFlashSale
on the train back from Scarborough
on a whim the morning after
you let me spend two full days
in a big tent you'd bought
for your daughters

in the many years we weren't together
I went to a lot of bleak places
but in Crewe
even Poundland had given up the ghost

I hotfooted it
to the cultural melting pot
of the award-winning train station

Loom Room, Blackburn

in the room were five looms
and a marbled sculpture of a woman with a boob
that I snapped on the sly and surreptitiously sent to you

the two receptionists looked startled when I entered
I'd seen two tower blocks in the distance
but they didn't seem worth walking to
in the rain   the museum was dry
and I thought there might at least be paintings
of factories to look at here

why don't you take a look at the looms?
urged the man
all cobwebs and memories
who manifested from behind them

the top two floors were closed
due to a problem with the roof

We've got a magnificent collection of coins,
an unparalleled assortium of beetles. We don't need
London. London even borrowed our coins once, Ha!

I was quickly done in there
the history was the usual sort
and conventionally displayed

There was a time they came from all over the world
to Over Darwen. It's proper name. The chimney there
is older than the Venetian chimney it was based on
in the end, so —

it's nearly closing
he gets lots of things out   of a special drawer for me

the large collection of old spinning machines and looms
are made even more interesting when the Room Steward
begins to explain their background and history

especially as   many years ago
he worked assembling them

there's a taxidermied dog on display
called Bed of Stones
        it was dying   got itself saved
went on to win some races   earn its way
into this fine cabinet

if we take a thing at its lowest and bring it back to life
should it be grateful for anything to which we expose it?

Ex Terra Lucem

for St Helen's

who told her we were giants, once?

– Fran Lock

last time
he made a swan
that's what she wants
the same again
she remembers more detail than really exists
how he put an eye on

we watch the glass roll round the stick
like some primordial marshmallow
like the girl's head is long and stretched
patted with burning black newspaper
like the trees are long and stretched
and hide the stretched head
our head that was on the television once

we are sometimes given monuments

it is 17 pounds 50 for a glass swan
in the museum shop

I want magic to happen

in the echo chamber we stamp our feet
while a man cleans the windows of the door
to the adjacent
        annexed
        consumed
        poorly lit
        downscaled local library

in many small-town Northern museums
we find quotes in jolly fonts
about very particular carbohydrates
                                        outdated slang
like what my father used to speak

maybe he still does

I've never seen her sit so calmly
without a screen
as when she watches the turning of the molten transparency
it took him half an hour to make a wavy dish
the bubble a tiny middling exhale

no one knows why Intestine City is called Intestine City
no one
but people are able to find a tiny piece of glass
from 2,420 years ago and explain it
from the earth comes light
we should not deny it

around Wigan Civic Centre is a fence
four little trucks are tilling the pavement
on the fence it says *CivicCivicCivicCivic*
like a bad file name

it's going to boast
Modern Creative Workspaces
for a range of start-ups and growing businesses

she wanted the glassblower to make a vampire
he was only ever going to make a swan again

it'll be alright

but imagine if ambition needs a furnace
by which I mean the funding for a furnace
mummy doesn't have a furnace
by which I mean the network to secure a furnace
    by which I mean a future
    by which I mean a job

we don't even have the funds
regionally
to maintain old dreams of dolomite

Looks Like a Crunchie

in late-stage Swansea
we weave around the ex-BT tower
dip into the oversized charity shop
on the retail park
then feel depressed about it

charity shops are facing increasing competition
from resale apps like Depop and Vinted

I remember a brass crocodile
on sale in Barnardos
in Knutsford for 25 pounds

items are priced according to what
customers in a certain area can tolerate

there's a huge new charity superstore in Bolton
        it laid out a red carpet on the day of its opening
everyone is talking about it
some of the items in there have been worn only once

customers could be forgiven for thinking
they were in a high-end fashion store

I want to hunt and gather

and though I do see the merits of connecting
the city to the bay, I don't want to move
in synchronisation with the illuminating facade
of an arena that pulsates with life, day and night

they've created a digital skin
to wrap around a pocket park
where   connecting the city to the sea
is a cutting-edge golden arch

but the bridge isn't gold
it's yellow
it's metal   to reference metal
it's got holes in the shape of swans

to reference swans
which in turn references the place we are in
though that's not even why it's called that
nor in that language

and we do a funny thing then
because the guardians haven't bothered yet
to take down the plans
we walk
toward the digital skin
curious about its Velcro buzz cut
that from a distance could be some brand
new world of exposed concrete
of showing it like it is

we get up close
and worse than the light shows of future
touring comedians
who are richer than us
but make us laugh about Pizza Hut and Ray-Bans
is a glowing membrane of colour
that doesn't work
or they can't be arsed to switch on

we aren't even compelled to touch it
which is not how I feel about Mount Fuji
or the frill of the ocean as it fizzles through sand
or my unfathomable, incessant children

we see the bridge
the shit bridge
throwaway as anything I might give
my kids to calm them

it has those funny holes in
deconstructed swans   to reference a deconstructed city

and through each hole a new perspective
future-facing   pointy
yet very much rooted in a sense of place and identity
because the view
through those spirited triangles and rhomboids
any of them
is very much still late-stage Swansea

the bridge design currently lacks
architectural quality and it appears
that the finer details and use of materials are unresolved

we cross the bridge
like walking through a Happy Meal
we come to the plans
how the plot was sold us
all the people of the world
mooching in sunlight

among these remaining cranes
among these wind-flung coke cans

If a shop receives a particularly valuable item, such as
a Versace dress, and it does not sell at a higher price,
rather than knock money off, charities will move the item
to another location where locals are more affluent
to maximise its sale price.

it's gone then
we won't think of it again

the park at least is experienced
briefly

Fifty City Centre Towers Built in the Last Five Years

and none
of them
are ours

none of
them are
the towers
we could
have been

High Point, Bradford

after Bradford & Bingley Building Society

it enters into a successful dialogue with its neighbours.
You value each more because of the presence of the other

– Architectural Review

if the unconscious is involved
in the design of the building
its knife-slash eyes
    mosquito-net Fontanas
keeping the prey at bay
    (but hold two palms together
    see what shape they make)

it was obvious
first thing I saw   (our eyes will go a certain way)
we know what we're looking for
(a truly Victorian self-confidence)

it was obvious
so obvious   they'd fuck us
        trifecta

    by taking the third away

if the unconscious is involved in the design
of a building then why don't we consult it
when we confiscate a place?

Just a Natural Consequence of Their Design, Just Part of Their Natural Life Cycle

it is strange to watch four towers blow up
in the fog
playing peek-a-boo like they knew
like they wanted the local papers to say

OUR MONOLITHS REMAINED UNTAMED TILL THE LAST

or

**IN TYPICAL FIDDLER'S FASHION,
THEY ARE GOING OUT ON THEIR
OWN TERMS**

the skyline afterwards was much the same
as it had been for most of the morning

amateurs in the crowd asked questions
such as *which ones?* and *where are they?*
while standing directly in the pantomime line
and we shouted back *behind you!*

on Facebook, Carl begged the ether
rather late in the day
if the demolition could be cancelled
because he couldn't see clearly
(the post was not reported)

a lady in a beret stood for three hours
in snow on the pavement by her tripod
far too far away to capture anything

I stared at the corner of a house
willing the hyberboloids to materialise
and darken, like a nude's underwear
on a mug that changes colour in heat

a cooling tower cannot be embarrassed
but it can be annihilated

a scar is the mark left when you destroy a thing
it is not the thing
a scar requires there to have been a removal
it exists in the after, reduced
to a worthy absence
it implies having missed, like Carl,
who stayed home in the end, the bulk of the action

as with any change of state, there is a pause
        our legs spin

we have chosen unknowing
we have chosen the cliff

the clouds did not part
but they thinned
same as how nothing is ever complete

it was 9:36 when Eris pressed
the button   a cable unsnapped
from the plastic block she was holding
like a gleeful hoover cord putting itself away

Eris has mixed emotions about winning the raffle
        with the comforting landmark gone
        how will she know when she's home?
her son is sad
the view from his bedroom window is changing

Eris doesn't mention her feelings post-initiation
she shares a video from her husband's phone

as a child I had a recurring dream
about winning a raffle I wasn't supposed to enter
and under the sudden storm clouds and hail
running away   my father's voice booming
like the crack of four towers coming down

the structure collapses like a thin chocolate shield
doused in hot liquid caramel
I put a chocolate ball like an oyster in my mouth
in the revolving restaurant where we would try to impress
the billionaire who eventually sacked us
and its form imploded
in one expensive second

this wasn't a failure though
I'd played my role

the towers fold like soft forms in fire
like kites caught in trees
like the fresh moves of inflatable men at car dealerships
being fanned through the knees
like pylons collapsing
like parachutes on top of my body   starved of wind

I want to watch the enormous shrink

photos of the four resultant chicken-pox stains
on the ground
make me gag
                        just dust now
we're ghosts inhaling the insides of hoover bags

the material keeps coming
it will keep on coming

they are designed to collapse into their own pits
not to disturb anything
to pop   in a footprint

this is a date, I said
and kissed your cheek

the fog was brown and orange like when the Sahara
comes and coats us

the pub was rammed
people were drinking Heineken in the street

The Top of the Tower Wasn't Visible in the Mist

a few hours later I screamed *I hate you*

I said *I don't want to look at houses*
we're not going to view
I said *I just want to see the pit*
from where I live
I said *I don't want slugs or damp*
or chunks of plaster coming away
if the children pull on the curtains
I said *I don't want a crack in the neighbour's wall*
dropping detritus onto a yard that could be
if anyone had time to nurture it, a garden
I said, when the towers came down, I said *now*
this is only half a thing
I said *the pub's got to change its name now*
I said *I can't look at the horizon now*
I said *how long will they keep us waiting*
I said *it's like a broken arm now*
I just want to get it over with

Penthouse

I want the view
from a distance

but that is not my life

Perpetual Night

if you don't like a thing because it's been neglected
then maybe you shouldn't have neglected it

it is hard to believe
that on the top half of this island
male architects could ever think less
sun was the answer
that what people needed
to help them shop
to guide them to the shops
was less light
more low-hanging dullness
they couldn't shift

after fifteen years, everything is fifteen
when they tear down Smallbrook in Birmingham
        a vote won 7 – 6

to replace it with three taller towers
with gaps between
what the guardians don't see is the same amount of light
still blocked, just flipped

I am pulled away from groups of boys
near beautiful air vents
when I'm interested   enough, I stop
being scared of things

outside the structure , an early death
I'm taking well-composed photos
though I'm not, myself, yet

beautiful, distant views emanate
from the penthouse
in a myth of trees

                                                    we can't undo anything
I'm speaking about an earlier injustice
some Victorian railing

Silo Auto

The first thing we went to see was the car park. Views are always free from the car park. You never fall out of use if you're a car park. People are in and out of you all day long if you're a car park. They keep your external walls clean if you're a car park. You get paid a decent amount per hour if you're a car park. Never any doubt about your function if you're a car park. No one questioning your aesthetics if you're a car park. What a big family you have, always visiting you, even on public holidays and Sundays, if you're a car park.

If the Building Is Like Me

i.e. not what was hoped for
semi-abandoned
rotten, forgotten
costly, high-maintenance, personally disliked
by a little over half the population
loved by a select few
held in disregard by many others

then why am I not free to walk here

Miami, Lyon, Trieste, (Budapest)

twenty years ago
we'd sit here for hours saying *hello hello*
waving and drinking wine
meant for cooking with
thinking nothing
of our lives
taking trams
buying Tibetan singing bowls and roller skates
and zipping around Beijing on the widest of pavements
in pink-gold trainers with dull orange laces
we'd bought from metropolitan flea markets
when our soles had fallen off
and been caught dragging on the pavement

I love wearing a thing
into the ground
and replacing it

the bar was covered in white slips of paper
declarations of love
movement records, data

the girl had a clutch of patches on her bag
displaying the names of cities
Miami, Lyon, Trieste

before I went to Budapest I emailed myself
the job description so I could go over it
ahead of my interview in the morning
after the late flight back
which I didn't really want to do
as these four days were for ignoring it
for swimming up and down the lanes in pools
steam rising, obscuring the view
getting my body out and not being concerned
because at forty-one it was more impressive
than at twenty-two
this persistent not dying
this running for transport

the woman at security had three names
tattooed on her forearm
Tiffany, Orion, Celeste

on the way to Budapest I dropped my daughter
to school
then ran for the bus, which was forty-one
minutes late because what they like to do
is conjure a schedule and then
it dissipates   *poof*

like time does for the poor
who live largely in queues
or under bus shelters with sideways seating
that my children can't balance on
and which prompt me
to explain to them the architectural
urban rules
in sideways rain
that soaks right through

in the end they cancelled my interview
before the beginning of it because they'd already found
someone to fill the role and what they wanted to do
Adobe, Flowdock, Pinterest
was source an easy bank of freelancers to use

much like the Community Connector position I didn't get
that turned out also to be a thinly veiled
have you thought about volunteering
a maybe we could catch up soon
a maybe you'd like to invest

I had an email a week after the interview that said:
We would love to find out more about your facilitation work,
your ambitions in this area
and how we might work together [without paying you].

much like the market research questions slipped
into the retail interview

my position is largely vulnerable   prone
to being ghosted

there were ghost children on the friezes
of grandeur-faded buildings
cherubs you said
but I wasn't feeling cute

my facilitation work has recently been very focused
on facilitating someone to employ me

we walked up and down the rising walkways
of a new structure that curved upward
like a miracle fish on your palm
made of sodium polyacrylate
and indicating only how sweaty you are

sculptural and overtly interactive
we walked up and around the structure's
stepped landscaped roof

it told us what to do
and we like that now
as people
we like museums that tell us when and how
to take pictures
we like to look at one painting then another
and if they could be grouped
according to chromatics or chronology
and ideally have all the themes pulled out too

we like to read the pocket-history plaques
that direct us to understand streets
in the ways others would like us to

I look at some balloons
they are big because we are supposed to be happy
with what has happened to our industrial warehouses
we are supposed to be satisfied
when we are ninety and female and the centre of attention
and very well paid
despite having locked ourselves up
for forty-seven years   and counting
to avoid certain questions

we are supposed to forget
the serious commentary
and just enjoy the visual experience
in a crowd
in an allocated time-step

over the course of a couple of months
I keep seeing the same tentacle
with a different acquaintance in front of it
like some mad collective dream on a loop

this is your art degree
this is your art degree

you will buy these trousers

in the bar with the paper slips
declaring love affairs and swearing at things
we looked for our city, the past
anything of merit
you said a lot of men
when given a pencil
can only write the names of football teams

two bored musicians sang American Pie
and Hotel California
and some other shit
while a coked-up Brit moved his body around
in a Crazy Frog T-shirt for the camera-phone lens
of his tight-lipped girlfriend
and clinked whiskey glasses
na zdrowie, to us, terviseks!
with the local relaxing alpha who was one of the few people
awarded one of the not-enough tables in the room

I apologised for making you go there
but sometimes we want to see
what has happened to our memories

it does make you wonder though
if it was shit then too
not the city
but how an outsider is conditioned to interact with it

I didn't know Budapest had a castle
I think I've been there six times
I haven't always done what I was supposed to do

we took the metro to the cogwheel railroad
looked at but did not stay in Hotel Budapest
with its breathtaking views
its fifteen floors above the city in the shape of a circle
offering a unique panorama from all the rooms
its retro character reflected
in the interior architecture and furniture
its spiral walkway ascending around a hanging column
of mahogany-framed mirrorlets
tinted like rum

there's a lot of dust
the fridge doesn't work and the windows
do not have handles on them
there was a storm and I didn't know how to close them
so a young man at reception gave me a spoon
I wish this was a joke
but the breakfast is nothing special and a mess

two boys in the plunge pool
haven't completed the plunge pool
until they've tolerated it for longer than us
than me
they tell us about a party on a boat that lasted all night
and until 5am
I tell them about morning trains being cheaper
than hostels
twenty years ago
and about drum and bass clubs and mistakes and children
and you whisper to me, *I am forty-three*

later, in the steam
which is like an intrusive thought but foggier
one of them finds me again and says *hello*
which is like being accepted for a second interview

I nod and look malleable, shoehorning in my referees
and my ability to work childcare around the demands
of the position and how Budapest has been at the forefront
of my plans and my dreams for now and for all time

I make you give me a piggyback in the water
because I enjoy slight social embarrassment and I want to be a child

in the field with all the Soviet statues
we discuss if at any point they will merit protection

you say the bronze will outlast the concrete
you say everything we like
is from the 1970s

I try to squint at the buildings
or crouch
or just not look at the internet
but I remember getting a veggie burger in Budapest
that was just an apology and a leaf

when I worked in Poundland in the late 1990s
we'd clean the floor
with a dustpan and brush
three aisles of carpet
down on our knees

not all the kids worked
I thought it was liberating
that financial independence
a sign of maturity

the first electric portable vacuum cleaner was invented
in the nineteen hundreds

I don't want to join a preservation society, I don't
I just want to persist
in the steam
in the mist
until we are somebody else's discovery
and they campaign for the plaque
on the Turnpike Library in Leigh
or by Atherton Train Station
in Manchester West
that will tell us what they think we mean

Unproductive and Unfunctional Blankness

it was a twenty-mile walk
or thereabouts
and I began by getting on the wrong bus

there are two buses to choose from
the number is usually on the front

a lot of the time I don't pay any attention
yet remain utterly convinced
that the world is against me

I ran fifteen minutes to get back to where we started
because my friend had travelled from Newcastle
on the promise of a good time

after 1.5 hours we'd been in Tesco
to buy sealed bags of wet chestnuts

    we passed my mum's flat
    I considered nipping in

the walk is starting now, I said
clocking what time the sun fell
    we're fast, don't worry
    we'll make good progress after this bit

we walked the wrong way up the canal

it wasn't entirely clear who was in charge of the map
or which app, if any
we were using

it is very hard to escape the place of one's birth

eventually we wandered into a field

there was no track, sometimes a dog
sometimes the distance sound travels
between the nearest traffic and a place where no one is

maybe twenty years ago I imagined being a Roman
while walking along some undulating track
on a hilly incline in mid-North Cumbria

really imagined it

when you walk through a field
or across an airport runway
or to a huddle of cooling towers
outside Widnes
from relatively far away on a murky Thursday
because you are unemployed and sick of asking
for the same thing
you can start to appreciate scale

a horse reared
behind a low fence

signs started to imply we shouldn't be here

I hate guard dogs
the way they ruin an entire species

if you enter a cafe near a bus interchange
in Warrington and ask for a flat white with oat milk
in mud-slopped, nebula-patterned leggings
old hiking boots, and with your hair
the victim of both indifference and a storm wind
people have trouble
knowing what bracket to put you in

you're nothing in a field

I want to scream *I've walked here!*

I'd like to know my face
only from casual encounters
in the lull of an otherwise rushing stream

I am always pleased when I pass an animal
safely

I asked the woman
who emerged from the shed
not if it was her land
            that didn't interest me
but if this was a trail
by which I meant a path
not if it was picturesque
but if I could pass

she said no, which I think meant she didn't understand
the question
she said there was nothing that way
by which I think she meant only fields
she said you won't know where you are going
which I'd tried to make clear didn't bother me

it is hard not to exit a field
the way you are told to exit a field
by the owner of that field
in the presence of the owner of that field

she said there was a fence to the left
and thumbed us towards it
she said, *it isn't really used* and looked irritated
like when you have a car crash on a cold bank holiday Monday
at 5pm, and instead of home
there's likely to be hours of death-lashed admin

we were ten-minutes by car from my house by this point

it took us a while to scale the wall by the locked gate

opposite the car park to the garden centre
that attracts over 1 million visitors annually
and for which the son of the founders, lucky sod,
received a lifetime achievement award
for his contribution to the garden retail industry
I did wonder what I was doing with my life
and what my children would eventually make of me

the walk is starting now, I said
clocking what time the sun fell
we'll make good progress after this bit

Retail and Entertainment Complex

many are the times I have stood
before a broken automatic door
waiting for it to open for me

you told me to write a poem
about the Trafford Centre
and this is it

You Get Free Parking All Day

the word *community* is stuck on repeat
on a broad banner in the centrepiece of Runcorn
there is no rain here   in here
we are safe from the weather

there is no one here really
the pub is closed

little trees have been popped at the bases of all the stairwells
so we don't notice the stairwells and attempt to ascend

they don't want us to be reminded of what was once
dreamt for the upper level

we've got to ignore the fact we are all ashamed

in Car Park A, a couple
are selling upright crystals from the back of their van
someone is presenting a battery-powered hamster
mimicking sentient movement inside a translucent sphere
someone is hawking a DVD we've all seen and cannot play

my mother has been decluttering her flat
for the best part of a decade

rows of lights are arranged
to attract us   a train, a santa, a reindeer with shades
Take a selfie here.
        and they *are* doing
        it's Christmas

show them
tell someone   this is premium retail space

Smoothie

I give all my buildings sensational nicknames so I can take a little bit of them home with me.

You were talking about the Roger Stevens building in Leeds with one of your direct reports and you nearly called it *Smoothie*.

Smoothie is dozens of Mini Milks around a block of Marseilles soap. A creamy slip of snail mucus. Candy-flossed wool fat rubbed against hips. Trails down a wet back. A bathroom puffed with steam.

I'm walking around Smoothie singing *Smoothie O Smoothie*. It is beige and atrocious.

I'm touching it.

A year later, I'm on a treasure hunt around the site. Twenty of us, looking for hidden artisanal tiles crafted in the Brutalist style. *Big Rog*, our guide for the day says, gooey-eyed. I am not the only one to pet-name buildings.

They put a little house over there, which I didn't expect to see, at the base of the broad, yellow-edged podium, by the slab lake of our poor region's unloved Barbican, and the walkways they've closed off to us now, because it's always our fault, we're so stupid, we ruined it, why couldn't we behave anywhere, take care of anything?

Imagine If My Life

had been designed with viewing platforms, or shared public spaces threaded through with dynamic walkways across gentle melting pots for original ideas.

Imagine if my life was an extroverted three-storey lending library, curving out beneath a larger eight-storey reference section that formed a bold inverted ziggurat, one of only two such examples in the world. If it had been formed of concrete planes floating above pillars now encased in glass, lending the top-heavy shape an improbable weightlessness. My vast interior low-ceilinged and cool, untouched by direct sunlight.

Imagine if my life was the most notable component of a tired concrete and glass complex, characterised by rough sleepers and graffiti, secret squares, dead ends, and grimy passageways.

If my life was remembered for its determination to create a coherent visual image by non-formal means, emphasizing visible circulation, identifiable units of habitation, and fully validating the presence of human beings as part of the total image, to the point that this human presence almost overwhelmed the structure.

Just imagine if my life had been heavy and immovable, yet artistically sculptural, and reliant on depth to create patterns and compositions with shadow and light.

Used strong, bold shapes. Was gigantic and sought to dominate its environment.

Imagine if my life bore little or no relationship to its older neighbours. If it was sublime, delicately terrifying at times. Tailored to not only function beautifully but also to delight and stimulate the senses.

Imagine if an attempt to save my life drew an outcry from high-profile architects, who banded together to ask that I be revitalized.

Middlehaven

If you don't like it, knock it down. Knock it down again. Just keep knocking it down until you get it right. My child does this with a pack of cards, her hands full of dice.

This is my home. I have bought it and I will keep on buying it.

A metallic college wall, overgrown fields like willing triangles of skin, two bold hoops stretching nothingness into two final indifferent interjections in the landscape that you must keep looking at, and a casualty of rail.

BOHO SCRAPHEAP answers the corrugated metal edifice between the abandoned town-hall hull and the regenerating generation plant going on generations beyond its means.

Bohouse is designed to offer flexible space to allow you to work from home and set up your new business in the digital and creative industries.

Imagine looking out of this onto how many times they told you no and made you start again until you stupidly adhered.

The Possibility of Extravagant Passage

Inside the Crystal Maze Experience, it's all running and corridors and going between things. Pipes and fire-exit signs and indistinct metal cylinders and exposed booms and shaky camerawork.

At the 1936 Olympic Village in Berlin we ran from the security guard, who seemed largely disinterested.

In my dreams I'm in a hotel with a convoluted lift system next to a flyover next to a big wheel next to a contested structure.

At Manchester Airport, when we were delayed, you said let's walk to the end, then let's walk to the other end. We sat in a vacant room with two hundred blue seats and photographed each other waiting on them.

On the elevated concrete around Bonny Street Police Station in Blackpool, we were dressed well and old enough, so only lackadaisically hounded.

In my childhood, we were in what I now know as Forton Services drinking Coca Cola from large plastic cups emblazoned with the words *Coca Cola.* We took them home like prizes before branded merchandise was commonplace.

Before the Institute of Science and Technology at the UMIST campus, a site whose cohesion and integrity have already been degraded, the two security guards I know by face asked if I was lost again.

In my mind, I'm revolving.

On the beach with my daughter, she puts her feet in our sand holes and we pretend she's a weed breaking concrete.

In Belarus, my host said I am taking you to the third object.

The third object was a colossal space. An eight-foot hook hanging in the middle. And on one of the staircases a security guard, so we escaped.

We spent Easter Sunday in the mouth of a grabber like untended baby birds and rolled about on the rails.

Whenever I try to turn into anything circumstances take me away.

By circumstances, I mean systems of control.

I bought a T-shirt that said I was a failure on it, so at least I could own something.

In Warrington, after the explosion of the four northern cooling towers, I wrote to the site owners. Said, I'm a poet, can I come in? They said, of course not, there are active explosives, then they entered the minefield.

I dug my hand deep into the still-warm ground of the recently erupted volcano. Everyone was doing it.

I don't live close enough to grieve these towers. I avoid eye contact at the blowdown in case I'm called upon to identify other local landmarks.

In my dreams, whales bash about me in choppy uncontainable pools. The strength, the scale, their ratio to my lack of consequence. The threat remains close, alluring. These dreams are situated in a completely distasteful gentrification of Akureyri, an Icelandic town whose economy, in the dream, is built entirely around and for this spectacle.

Chanel came to Manchester and left again. Dismantled their covered walkway. It was all over the news, that walkway. *The Chanel Tunnel.* Intended as a temporary structure, for insurance reasons they couldn't let us keep it. They'd contextualised their tweed and now they were on their way. Said we could have the bits though. If we had the will to reassemble. Dumped them in a warehouse nearby. Saved them the bother of disposing. Now we pay for the bits and don't do anything with the bits because the bits remind us of not being cared for.

We will never admit this.

In the business district of Milan, the statue of the middle finger by Maurizio Cattelan, after much deliberation, and being eventually donated by the artist, was declared permanent.

In Stockton the giant bauble says *Stockton Sparkles.*

In Stockton

I go into the tourist information office
because I need a fridge magnet
it is a vast empty space
that recalls grand boutiques of Nespresso capsules
in all the colours of the universe
that all taste the same

three members of staff jump up
to find me a fridge magnet
there must be a fridge magnet
but they only have Yarm
and that is not at all what interests me

I buy a print of Billingham

the main member of staff apologises
for what she feels
is overcharging

I ask what sights we can take in
but she says, in walking distance?
there is nothing

directly outside the shop is a steampunk automaton
that rises from a plinth at 1pm every day
when not obscured by a shiny reindeer
and she didn't think to mention it

there are grubby portholes in the plinth
through which the machine can be glimpsed

Stockton
despite being dubbed a shithole
has knocked out all its surplus retail space
to make way for an urban park
for an opening out

people will be able to walk uninterrupted
to the riverside from the high street

the Wobbly Goblin nightclub
has invited any Tory MP to come and experience
Stockton's *lively beats and vibrant scenes*

the life expectancy of women
in Stockton
is the lowest in the country

the Stockton Flyer Train is stuck halfway in its plinth
and appears to be broken

is it on strike?
does it work for Northern Rail?

Split 3

Mirko dropped me. In the traffic. Eyes streaming. Trails of automobiles. *We are not* in *traffic, we* are *traffic.* I keep remembering this. Velebitska ulica. My life is great and in bits. A piecemeal Stari Grad. A starry grid. Dirty old town. A half-understood thing.

The project was abandoned in the eighties. It never went down to the sea. The university library. Glass. They tried. (We tried.) I walk behind walls, poke out of the grass. Bulk. Filler. Highrises, like so many structural uncertainties, waver in the noncommittal coasting wind.

Old lady on a bench. Old man on the steps. High heel. Concrete. Handbag. Recess. Goth in a pale dress. Purple windows iridesce in sliding lightlessness. Dive bar under moon-orb streetlamp. Pool. Flood. Metal gates. Peephole punctuations dot roadover walkway. I wish you were here with me. It is okay to dream things.

Pujanke: Pull it. Jank me. Visoke: This will be okay, I think.

They started to have ideas again. High above the city. The centre was a palace, walled little heart there. Ornate, pink.

Split 1: Historical, loved, predictable, tended.

Split 2: Entropy. City as spill.

Split 3: Necks pecking. Cranes in heat. Boxes stacked too wall, too tall to fathom. Stand at the top and wait until the sides fold in. Vertigo. Verdant. Change begins on the hill. Dogs in cages. They are barking at anything not in cages. Kids will wherever you put them find a swing. Everywhere a barber. Frizer. Fresh air. The steps have all got cracks in.

I like the arrows on the roads. I like it when construction tells me where to go. Right angles. Blue and red *L*s suggesting what is going to be built. A self-contained apartment. Slot me right in.

Vents are gills. Silence spreads from the enormity of no-longer-new build. A smooth matte wall. Sink into the softness. The portal. Leave me a handprint. My body in plaster, in alabaster. Cast her. Always, you always should have asked her. Charcoal. Mud mask. Face paint. Sidestreet. Sinkhole. Quicksand.

Gravity. Erection. Helium. Utopia. Exurbia. Excavation. Disclosure. Explosion. Minefield. Name it. Never forget to put a name on the things you want to will. Madness. We can manage this. The proliferation. Hand me the blueprints, all the hope you forged this part of town with. Everything. We're a cute little wasteland. I will find unassuming corners where the shadows are long and thin in the evenings. I will find tiny pockets to put us in.

There are windows, doors. Narrow alleys. A tree where a slab has been relived. I hop over a fence. Drop down the steps. I turn a corner. Look over a low wall and see where the cars sit. Underneath. They wanted us to breathe deep, be peopled. The sun is shielded. It is cool in the portholes. Protected from extremes. We walk where we are guided. Trust the design. The balconies have curved frames. I am soft in the suburb. I am soft in this place we have made and believed in.

My eyes are your eyes. They are welling in the tight sunlight. My landfill. Bending like great metal structural beams that jut uncovered in patchy scraplands. Concrete blocks drying in heat. A lizard. A leaf. I nip through a car park. I want to be behind and inside elements first imagined then implemented. I too was first imagined before I became material. I too was once a precarious proposal trying to secure a deal.

Monuments. Moments. Monumental. Memorial. I am a highrise and you are a highrise that has been erected next to me. No space between. There's a shared wall. A party wall. The weather in time will discolour our sleek external sheen. Chosen textures. A surface. I will melt in the kiln. Remember when they thought the world would be better than this? I walked from Pujanke down to the sea. I had faith in the plan, and the gentle human forms of the city fed me to the undefinable murkiness of water. Huge cubes of specified function. Agency. A city drops like rain on solid grit. Remember me. Take my hand and design something.

Born Into It

Imagine always wanting a baby, then having a baby, and then being told, upon having that baby, that you're not allowed to talk to it or help it in any way. Most importantly you are not allowed to replenish anything that may become depleted. And there you have the Right to Buy Scheme.

save the southern towers / convert to trendy dwellings / pub's changed its name already / looks so sad / flying into Liverpool / all four of them / looks like Fiddler's Ferry is going to be in this / the low cloud making it look as if they were still working / might stay up and watch it / the modern-day equivalent of public executions / is anyone else missing them / snapped this on my way to the local / a couple of staff members are thanked in the credits / first sighting post-op / unpalatable / an entire typology risks being wiped out / you lads may not like this post / an entire industrial building type / I have some good memories / mixed emotions for raffle prize winner / I was a contractor for many years / I was really surprised to have won the raffle / contractors were a big part of every power station / from new build through to and including demolition / I try to tell my missus and kids what it was like / I've never won anything before! / but I can't find the words / my kids have seen the eight towers every day on the way to school / half of my whole life is gone / it has been a special interest for my son for years / mist obscured the view / she goes down in history / great ingenuity was taken to integrate them into the surrounding countryside / he knows so many facts about it / with Henry Moore advising on their placement at Didcot and Sylvia Crowe writing extensively on the subject / so he's been excited but also sad they won't be there anymore / a comforting landmark / I'm really grateful / only 29 individual towers remain / for winning the raffle / not sufficiently distinctive to merit protection / grown up fascinated by them / all pre-war examples have now been demolished / people know they are home when they see it / welcome to the public consultation for the first phase of Fiddler's Ferry / I was standing here when I had my profile picture taken / this interactive website will guide you through the proposals / superb expressions of the engineer's art / at the end we will ask you to complete a short survey / hopefully a few travellers will go there this weekend and the demolition will get suspended for a few more months so we get more time with them / emblematic of post-war modernising ambitions / I went there on Saturday and it looks mad / these heroic titans of industry deserve better / I know plenty who, in times past, longed for it to go / been a week without them now and I'm still not used to it / hot, sweaty, dirty, enclosed spaces / scrap-carrying, refurb, welding, grinding, cleaning, it was an awesome job / there is something elementally graceful about the way they make heavy concrete visually light through a tender hyperboloid curve / your views really matter to us / I was sat on Spice of India car park today and I had a strange feeling / we are excited to share our initial plans / bet it will affect their take-ins now, as people went there because of the cooling towers / the power station's memory will live on / met some great people there over the years / these shapes are unlike any previous man-made structure, their scale and lines of construction link them with the mind and the forces of the universe / like I say, awesome job / the consultation is now closed, but comments and suggestions are still welcome / behemoths / a Certificate of Immunity (COI) is a document which guarantees that a building will not be statutorily listed (added to the National Heritage List for England (NHLE)) or be served with a Building Preservation Notice (BPN) by the local planning authority for the succeeding five years / I remember a few times needing the cooling towers myself / cooling towers were one of a number of revolutionary new shapes necessitated by mass electrification / will be sadly missed from the skyline / grade: not applicable / looks so sad / crashing down in a matter of seconds / not bothered / if you go back far enough you'll find the legend / by 2016, the station had already been making a loss for two years / Amber Rudd / Robert Byrch / it will be so strange when they are gone

Another Piece of History Flattened

you're nothing in a field

eventually

I wandered into a field

Sometimes All You Need is Someone to Make a Case For You

the Guild Hall is another one
they want rid of
it's all so difficult
keeping a thing alive

I walked up and down the main street
crying, like a cat trying to conceal its piss
looking for the right place
to land it

it is hard to please everyone
but some people know
how to command a room

*

command and commend are fused

we commit the person to our care
and then we own the room

*

but in the beginning was care

*

when you have the language
you can fight for that which is not in the rules

*

from Latin *commendare*
to commit to the care or keeping (of someone), to entrust to

from *com-*, here perhaps an intensive prefix
as in *come, come, I'll look after you*

and from *mandare*
to commit to one's charge

because one *is* in charge
and it isn't you

*

at least once a year
for most of my adult life
my rooms have commanded me
to exit

I am obedient
obedience is an important value

we turn up on time for work
for the most part
twiddle our thumbs in empty rooms
until the beds we have found online
are brought to us in cars as favours

we don't steal from hotels
though almost
we pay for the things we are asked to
when prompted

we consider the terms of our parents' employment
as they try to contain and command us

*

you're going to continue making mistakes
if within the structure there is no wiggle room
to improve

*

a friend lost her job selling insurance
at the Co-operative Group
for being too kind to the elderly

we thought it was funny at the time
how shit the world was

we watched year-end reports that mocked it
then mocked us
for egging on that mockery

*

since 2017 people have liked this bus station
seen it differently
some portion of that
is because they have been told it is again okay to

*

in the café in Heysham the girl wanted iced coffee
a freshly squeezed orange juice

they didn't have either
because not everything needs to be cosmopolitan
or efficient
or even very good

so she got her own food out

the café owner lost her rag at that
the entitled youth

for an hour then (and no doubt then some)
this narrative continued
to command the room

and with each retelling
bolstered as it was by local support
they had their allergy sign up, look!
she could been have catered for
she was taking up a table for four

with each retelling
it became a thing we wanted more of
the slight change in phrasing
the exact same phrasing

the iconic up-curved balconies
the Pirelli rubber floors
the hand-crafted iroko wood
the typography of the signage
    that Rail Alphabet typeface

this building is a *gesamkunstwerk*
every part pulls in the same direction
a coming together, like concrete

curdled, congealed

*

in the beginning there was care
small leaves in pairs that are almost nothing
but millions

the bus station was intended to be the nerve centre
of a suitably Lancastrian new city
Redrose

but
plans erode under orders

    crescendo
    concrescere

condensed, hardened, stiff, clotted

*

let's say we want that which is
material and is not abstract

let's say we are coming together
let's say we do

@PrestonBusStation

are following me on Instagram
they like a lot of my photos of buildings

but they didn't like the ones
of Preston bus station
I posted recently

too close to home, perhaps

The Ring Road Will Survive Us

It's beautiful, I said.
He didn't hear me.

What?
That building, I pointed, it's lovely.
Yes, he said, and started to tell me everything
he knew about the beautiful building
next to the one I was looking at

with its sad grey facade
demolition-ready
trying to appear like it always wanted to be
a B&M, a ping-pong parlour, a Vapenation,
a Poundbakery.

Holding its skirts up over its banisters.
A leak in the ceiling, a hole in the wall.
Not to be pretty or gracious or gentle.

If we make it look like a church,
if we make it look like a library?

Some curve round the ring road, wrap themselves
up in the safety of ring roads.

Above the garter glare of shop signs,
the illuminations are dying.
They stay on all year now,
desperate, cloying.

The act of being there, doggedly.

Jogging on One of the North West's Two Guided Bus Ways

there is something very sad about rushing
to a place before it is scheduled to be torn down

like how you tell me we have a good thirty years
together and I accept the blanket
misery before I do the maths again

my body quickly recovers
is happy to have passed a test

good little body   it likes to be tested

Axe Man

my daughter said first the plants
and then the fish and then the monkeys
stood up tall and then we built all this

Robert Moses, a man whose projects were responsible
for transforming large parts of the New York area
and revolutionising the way cities in the US
were designed and built said *when you operate*
in an overbuilt metropolis, you have to hack
your way with a meat axe

We Will Use Everything Eventually

I dip around the corner and it's gone
the enormous printer   *so ahead of its time*
that we photographed in the wind
for the Leftfield business cards
with the paper billowing from its enormous outlet

and my friend tugging on it
theatrically tugging on it
pulling away like an arrow or parallelogram

last night I had a dream about all the words starting
with *para* and the natural accumulation of language

paradigm, paranoia, parameters, parapet
paradise
parasite

there's pink in the window   bedsheet crimson
instead of a curtain
it winks at me like the pink of an entire street
because the guardians can do that if they want
in Salford
they can commission some artists to intervene
make a temporary and marketable wildness

who's looking after us?

there are cobbles   a full road's width
we will keep something   and call it a brick

the café is an estate agents
selling unfinished houses
from where the students used to eat

another accidental gated community

you will walk across silt
and like it

you will wait at the traffic lights
at the bus stop
exist between these roundabouts
your name will be lost on a list for sixteen months
or twenty years

the first time I entered the Irwell Valley Campus building
it was the second
tallest building I had ever been in
there was a "Tree of Knowledge"
on the wall of a 1960s tower block
they called a campus
because they were trying to convince us
we could make it

the artists weren't anywhere
near the rest of the students

we hovered over a bunch of locals
who didn't want us
not quite near enough to a peer group
who didn't want us

in my dreams
there is always an exhibition on the top floor
an open studio
I am still creating things
covered in paint with a thick head of hair
trials on acetate
an overhead projector

give me space
endless materials

I will stitch philosophical or irreverent quotes from books
into hundreds of pairs of functionless and badly made
knickers and drop them around Europe

no one will ever know if I mean anything by it

The Tree of Knowledge was saved
from the bulldozer at the 11th hour
one wall left standing for fifteen years
behind closed gates
without a building to lean on

the creator of that particular piece
in his 70s and living in Paris
said he was 'delighted' to hear
his work had been saved
an important part of Salford's cultural heritage

I dip around the corner
of Blandford Road
and it's gone
I know it's gone
yet I gasp   as I meet the goneness
because I've never felt it
because I've never been back
because there's nothing there to summon

just some unbuilt houses
built for everyone and no one

The International Council of Shopping Centres

before the thing got a chance to be listed
the guardians wrote to the government
and said, hey, can you protect this thing
from protection please, we've got a vested interest

whoever tells the story tells the story
anything else is just defence

the narrative is a fast-flowing river
that runs beneath our roads and under the railway lines
it is polluted so we try our best to ignore it
in the river are shopping baskets and shoes
and wheelie bins
in the river are bottles of wine and tomorrow
and a sequence of similar years and spalling concrete
and the best interests of our children

we cannot blame anything in the river
for being in the river
nobody started the river
it just goes

sometimes
as with art, as with the archive
you can see it there, retrospectively
and realise what has been done
it will look the way it did in the beginning
before weather, before cladding, before profit
and other forms of advantage
nudged the vantage point

the narrative is a brick-slip panel
and everyone is on the clock

how many bathrooms do you want
and who will fork out for them to be refurbished
do you cut your daughter's fingernails, coat her
these are important questions

we do not want to be the biggest house
main road or not
we do not want to be the eccentric purple door

as much as we might want to live in a tilted cube
on a stick
we don't go through with it

nor do we want to be idyllic
because it never is

we believe in the beating heart

we believe in renewal
in the perennial
in jacking it all in

we will change what we need to change
to maximise growth
we will utilise our environment
we will highlight the finest local food and drink

we know who we are
the centre has been ours since we first realised
we could do this

is it better to be used
to get used to being used
or to not be of use any longer?

we lack flair
we ourselves have displaced earlier versions
we too are guilty of inaction
of being boring and repetitive
and unexemplary

I will spend the rest of my life with you
we will watch them blow up everything

Heliocomplex

Today I approached the object that has been on the right for most of my life. I sat on the top deck with my finger over the buzzer. I thought, I'll press when it rears its ugly head. I pressed on the roundabout and I had to go down then. My eyes are two full reservoirs that life has pissed in and must be drained. We're gaining height; the city elongates like a finger trap from which no tourist can escape. School children don't know what to make of the outlying architecture; it is vague and exceptional. The city envelops me. I say thank you and step out. I like to turn to the edifice and direct my body as if controlled by it. In my dream I was up against the wall and then he left and then you came. I will apologise to no one. The walkway whirls like soft ice cream from an industrial apparatus into a cone we will take home and devour. My child ends up with it all over his face. I slide down the walkway as if enchanted. A boy on a bike conceals the blood on his face with his hood and his hand and I choose to believe him.

Here You Do Not Have to Imagine the Missing Seventy Percent of the Original Masterplan

But you can if you want. You can do whatever you like here. You can have a baby. Or not. No one is going to make you live up to any sort of ideal. Nor will they quote past theory or refer back to original design briefs. The space is organic, like you, like me, and the architect is living on the top floor, all glass, naturally, with an indoor pool around an indoor tree. There is a giant hand, as you can see, sometimes open, or sometimes, as a physical embodiment of negative space, as the tangibility of our tension, our mistakes, sometimes in the shape of the inside of a fist. He's keeping a diary; the latest residents have told him they are fine with everything. On the first day, someone said can I jump from here, can I throw a TV? Yes, of course you can. What you'll notice in these external embellishments is how it wears its vents on its sleeves. It's an architecture of maintenance. You can do what you like, as I say, we're not monitoring it. I'm sorry. I can't come in. No. I'm not at all interested.

Buildwas

I thought about getting a tattoo
of some cooling towers

I'm trying to find the structure I want
to be the one that is really mine
but it's hard to know
like anything
if permanence would ruin it

I've been wearing the same necklace since 2013
it's a fluke
but has been mistaken for many things

I got a sperm whale
tattooed on my calf recently

Sophie, an Ironbridge power station fan
left heartbroken by their demolition
has a tattoo of the Buildwas towers on her leg

Sophie said when she was misbehaving
or couldn't sleep
her mum would take her down to the chimneys
as she referred to them

Sophie said how can you regret it if it means something

at least when they're gone she can look at her leg
and see that they're still there

There May Be Close Contact

when we ran up the steps to the baths
you found the plaque
36 other pits would have been seen from here
something like that
poking out like those three objects in the water
at Port Talbot
like a huge chunk of Azerbaijan
as I walked from the airport

  digging into the ground
  sucking the stuff out

you said look at the flame
look at the flame
an open flame
it's just shooting up there
there would have been loads here back in the day
soon there won't be an open flame anywhere

I thought why
have I never been down a pit before

I remembered a mud cave in China
a salt mine in Poland

the mining museum near my house
has a very cheap café
in a marquee
I think they told me they needed to raise a million
just to keep the thing from falling down
how many marathons would that be

the pit head

my friend said his dad used to climb up and spin it
and people thought it was haunted
in the paper

in the gift shop of my little pit
that I watch from my kitchen
like my past has never been anywhere
else but inside me
I say I used to play here
on the carts
at night
up and down the rails
she says I'm not the only one
(I don't ever want to be the only one)

I imagine there are mountains in countries
where for generation upon generation
you can totally know the landscape

at Pwll Mawr
which sounds to me like a talon yanking
at a young mammal's face
I say I'm from Manchester
instead of Astley or Tyldesley

you berate me for that
a missed opportunity

but if you are from certain areas
you are sort of preconditioned to not be
entirely proud of it

The Remaining Group of Four

just hope this time they do it when they have better weather
as well
so people can see it unlike last year
as well
people paid out for a hotel nearby
as well
strange
they were upset after that
strange
as well
I wondered when the main smoke stack would come down
as well
strange
as well
the old Royal Liverpool Hospital is coming down
as well
strange
ah well
both were built around the same time

Archaeologists Scour Land

when I looked at where I could afford
to buy a house and realised I had to go back
to where I'd come from
I thought I'll take a look at what I've been avoiding

I found Tudor frontages in Wigan
slight hills, red and brown constructive tightness
cobbles and monuments
and tiny retail units all stacked up
thirty up, thirty down

I thought Leigh doesn't have one of these
all these little pockets of local possibility
I thought sell me a mug, sell me a hand towel
sell me a homemade earring, a candle, a book, anything
just stay with me

I want miniature doors, sharp corners, secret passageways
that sort of journey

I want people to start doing something
 baking a cake and putting it on a table

I want someone I know to make me a mini skirt
with a geometric print

I want a second-hand bookshop
to remain open in my town
on a pay-what-you-can basis
despite the appearance of a permanent occupier for the space
on a long-term lease

I thought Wigan is okay
the buildings look better as I age
maybe I'll start coming here for the day
wandering around these tiny shops
pointing my face at their little displays
remarking on how they ebb and change

a year later I moved home
got a job in Wigan
said to you shall we drive to Wigan
have a little look around Wigan
there was this one bit that pleased me last time
it was small and multiple, familiar and fluctuating
anonymous and not
where I felt both in the middle of the action, surrounded
and also very safe
like on the main square in Marrakesh
where all these small-scale historical things
are constantly happening to all the lives that linger
we throw hoops at 2-litre bottles of pop

not The Galleries, you asked
but I didn't know

we walked around Wigan

and I tried to find it

In Death the Problem Child Becomes Heroic

in Freudian therapy you have free association
and the person in therapy just talks
and actually what I didn't realise is that the analyst isn't supposed to
come to conclusions, just to listen
so it kind of becomes one unconsciousness talking to another
unconsciousness, bypassing intent
the key is in the irrelevant details
and after a period of listening the analyst might hit on something
once the two brains have become attuned
and might be able to make sense of something hidden in the details
so I think that the environment does this to us
it infiltrates how we build our selves
we are attuned
and it becomes absorbed into our character
depending on what we pay attention to
so I was always photographing walls that looked like they were crying
or lampposts that were talking to each other
or pylons holding hands
or a cheeky bollard
because the city is my imaginary friend

Plans to Transform Former Council Building into Gym, Cinema Room and Roof Garden

directly below the article
which shows the artist's mock-up
        like a green highlighter pen could fix it
like they drew some crisscrossing lines
and coloured them in
and said *very good* in a cocktail bar and thought
that will appease them

go Comic Sans on the proletariat

directly below the article
that indicates what the future thinks of the past
in certain areas
is a link to another article

am I going to die yet?

in Wigan

more people ask me where I'm from
than anywhere else on these islands
        they can't quite place it

when I was seventeen
a woman in a supermarket told me I was Irish
it isn't interesting
I said my mum is
I thought how does she know
it isn't interesting
I've just always wanted to be something

have you written any poems about Leigh?
a friend asked in the pub
like that cartoon lamb
with those cartoon eyes
that get bigger and bigger until we stop
eating them

I told him the guided bus way features in one

a cop-out perhaps
like going back to university
like closing down Oxfam

I just wonder if covering a building
in glass-reinforced plastic is always the best thing

when someone put gel acrylic nail polish
on my daughter's nails it took me weeks
to get it off again
and the nails were no better for the scraping

a guy in the IT department says it's ugly as sin
I say I'd be honoured to work
across the road from it
I say I arrive ten minutes early and loop around it
taking photos any time I'm sent here

the Civic Centre in Wigan

he says you should go to Stoke
I say I've been
I say Middlesbrough, Sunderland, Preston, Crewe, Billingham, Killingworth
I say, by the way, if anyone's ever getting rid
of that unlooked-at pastel drawing of the Civic Centre
in the corridor, I'll take it

I show him a photograph of the Turnpike Library
he asks is that here?
he says why do you like these things
I say this one was designed by William Mitchell
I grew up thinking that building was protecting me

I say this concrete
represents a long-dead utopian dream
in which it was morally necessary
to sanitise us
manipulate our movements

I say they won't replace it
with anything better
we're an experiment and we always have been

it was designed by two-time president
of the Royal Institute of British Architects

I say as friendships go together into the future
eventually the longevity
of that closeness becomes the purpose

    this curious warping in unison
    becomes the arm that links the sleeve

he tells me that though the new card reader
has a flashing light and weighs a few grams less
than its predecessor
and though it is a neat little palm-light quadrilateral
                    in fact
the old bulky, taupe tunnel of the previous
card reader
is the one to use
                              reliable and durable

I say *mhm*

he says
you're serious, aren't you?

Notes on the Poems

Looks Like a Crunchie uses text from a rejected planning application and various local newspaper articles about charity shops.

Imagine If My Life uses found text from such places as failedarchitecture.com, architectural-review.com, archdaily.com and europeanceo.com

In Stay Awhile, the phrase "there is something elementally graceful about the way they make heavy concrete visually light through a tender hyperboloid curve" is attributed to Otto Saumarez Smith, and the phrase "these shapes are unlike any previous man-made structure, their scale and lines of construction link them with the mind and the forces of the universe" is attributed to Sylvia Crowe.

Note on the Cover Image

"The Last Landmark" by Jen Orpin

"Forton Service Station has become an iconic landmark for travellers along the M6 motorway between Preston and The Lake District. Known for its distinctive tower, it stands as a nostalgic symbol of British road culture. Opened in the 1960s, Forton's unique architecture has made it a beloved stop and landmark for generations of drivers. It's this sense of familiarity and comfort on long journeys, evoking memories of past road trips and family holidays that has made it a perfect muse for my painting practice. This piece was commissioned by a regular traveller past Forton, it was the last landmark on his journey to visit his dad." —Jen Orpin, 2025

Web - jenorpinpaintings.com

Insta - jenorpinpainter

www.ingramcontent.com/pod-product-compliance
Lightning Source LLC
LaVergne TN
LVHW030922080826
845145LV00013B/3022

* 9 7 8 1 9 1 6 5 9 0 1 7 5 *